the art of forgetting

the art of forgetting

poems

andrei codrescu

Sheep Meadow Press
Rhinebeck, New York

Designed and typeset by The Sheep Meadow Press
Distributed by The University Press of New England

Cover image: William Kentridge, *World Walking*
Author Photograph: Brian Baiamonte

Library of Congress Cataloging-in-Publication Data

Names: Codrescu, Andrei, 1946- author.
Title: The art of forgetting / by Andrei Codrescu.
Description: Rhinebeck, NY : Sheep Meadow Press, [2016]
Identifiers: LCCN 2016003217 | ISBN 9781937679613
Classification: LCC PS3553.O3 A6 2016 | DDC 811/.54--dc23
LC record available at http://lccn.loc.gov/2016003217

All inquiries and permission requests should be addressed to the publisher:

The Sheep Meadow Press
PO Box 84
Rhinebeck, NY 12514

CONTENTS

MOTHER

UPLIFT

PRIVATE UTOPIA

ADAM WAS A TYPO

MOTHER

driving to see mom

We drove 2500 miles
to see my mother
we drove through five states
mostly on interstates
but when we couldn't take the boring
highway that unrolled like the crawl on CNN
for thousands of dull infinities
we took the smaller roads in the interior
of the united states of amnesia
and found many forgotten americas
some forgotten already one hundred years ago
some forgotten fifty years ago
some forgotten five years ago
some just forgotten
and we drove through towns that were being forgotten
as we drove through
we were quite possibly the last people to remember them
including the locals who had already forgotten where they lived
because they lived along an endless crawl
at the bottom of their screens

for 2500 miles I kept checking my iPhone's GPS
as if it knew better than the highway where we were going
and between directions I read that in China
my device was being made as we drove
"by 230,000 employees
many working six days a week
often spending up to 12 hours a day at the plant
over a quarter of them live in company barracks
earning less than $17 a day
the scale is unimaginable" an Apple employee said
and so were interstates in the united states of amnesia
where the crawl crawled at at the bottom of every screen

and when we finally reached my mother
we were in florida the state whose official flower
should be the opium poppy
and disney world "an unforgettable memory"

now what is it
exactly
we forgot?

when the stepfather died

when the stepfather died
my mother didn't know how to do anything
practical
he did everything online
he paid the bills online
the electric
the telephone
insurance
the security company
& the condo fees
the outrageously high fees for the condo
in one of those "adults only" florida compounds
where america stores its elders
and makes sure that they don't escape
several circles of vultures guard them
security gates
doctors' offices
banks
hospitals
surgery salesmen
driveby pill dispensaries
rehabs   lawyers   mortuaries
and not-so-free hundreds of channels cable tv

the stepfather died in the hospital
where he had been snatched from the jaws of death
several times at a cost only his insurance company knows for sure
when he died there was no more money in him
but my mother knew nothing of money
at 88 years of age she was closer to world war 2
than to the internet

she knew none of her neighbors
she had no friends
she had never availed herself of her adult
community's cinema
or swimming pool or clubs or the bus to the store
her job she explained was to take care of the stepfather
who was always online taking care of their business
when he wasn't in the hospital being repaired
so he could go back online

he died without telling her the password
or maybe she forgot that key-word that was or wasn't
his last word

for many days I reconstructed their finances
from a mountain of old papers
surely surely I thought there must also be hackers
around here

here is my only nugget of wisdom:
don't   do not   please don't
die with your password

dead husband

i'm not going to be a substitute
for the dead guy who was a substitute for me
even if i was made specially to be a substitute
for her father
all those other substitutes
were not specially made
they were just specially trained
some more specially than others
i am the rare one created for the job
with a kind of fierce craft that was the gift
of the first difference

ben Adam son of Eve

and now at the end when the last substitute
has vacated her bed and left for another world
i refuse the bed still warmed by its last occupant
who's laughing somewhere: he who laughs last etc
but i won't sleep in that big empty bed
"where the light is"
(according to Eva)

what's the point of being great
when all it means is finding out
what job you were made for

nothing to be specially proud of

in the refugee camp

40 years ago I took all of my mother's money in Rome to buy two fake gold
watches (unknown origin, marked Swiss) and today my mother whom I'm
visiting gave me unconscious rejoinder for my birthday: a fake gold watch
(made in China). Moral:
it takes four decades for a cloud
to go from wispy vague to shroud

mother

at the center of the cult: death
maternal umbilical strangulation
intact after half a century coiled
in worship of posters print tape
to which tolerated heirs came
joyfully mistaking the rites for high-
lights of their childhoods not knot
of darkness avenging a hurt womb

mother-actress

she is a very bad actress
but a better artist
but still not a great one
she made me so I could never leave her
and if I did and do it's because she wasn't all that great
she faked even my making

but she never counted on words
to be a better substitute for me
for refusing that for which i was made

"come see the light in the big room"

she was well loved though
many others were taken in by the charm
of her insatiable need

they were betrayed
she loved only the thing she made to love her
but didn't

if she had been a better actress
i might be feeling something of a fuzzy sort
instead of hyperlucidity

where she says

she can't live alone
she can't live without an enemy
she can't live without pain
alone means enemy pain is gone
who is kim?
who is kin?
her sentence
"I can't live alone"
is unfinished
the full sentence is
"I can't live alone
without someone to torture"
strangers are hard to torture
hospitality forbids it
until they stay the night

the photographer

In the old world, my mother was a studio photographer, a master of the pose. In the new world her snapshots are awkward. We look at them. Pictures don't lie—it's just that the people in them are lying for the pictures. That goes also for people looking at pictures—they lie about what they see. (Which is Nothing.) It was never Lumière's intention to challenge the power of real-world Shallow. How different is the quality of Shallow in photography! But how many dragon heads it has! I am one: my mother and father were both photographers, each with their own studio and cardboard sets. My head is not hard to chop off in today's motherless discussion. Genitors have their critical components, including exposure to the light. Light does not confine itself to sneer and inarticulation, it is a saber. Her photo studio challenged nothing: it treated equally dead old peasants, ID photos or police circulars. If her practice challenged an order it was that of orality. But it was a weapon specifically designed for dragons. The old camera with its curtains hiding her head was a troll under the bridge the dragon crossed every day on its way to school, its heads bobbing with the future. My own head, miraculously unchopped by commissars and theorists, stretched itself unmolested toward a lively exuberance. That was America. She never lived in it, I did.

assisted living

my 92 yr old mother calls to apologize
for ruining my childhood
i fixed that I say I became a poet
she calls 20 times a day doing a pretty
good job of ruining my old age

Top of Form

Bottom of Form

who was eva?

who was eva?

were her last words. born

january 24 or 26 1925 in alba iulia

in hungary then

her father was murdered

in the woods when she was 9

he owned a gold mine

to be safe she danced with nazis

she was the other

her sister cared for her mother

when the nazis fled i came

my father fled it was all the same

there were stand-ins

rehearsals for a part

in a school play with wings

i was the gold mine of death

for whom she hoarded things

she saved me for the end

to stand in for the fathers

i was not very far then

but already old

i turned down the part

you are not my mother

you are the lies she told

the last laugh

it only took three nights of insomnia
and a visit to the hospital to bring back
the dark universe of flat objects
the blizzard of commas semicolons points
moving on a flat plane always teasing
the intrepid adventurer to enter it
it was familiar   the screen-saver of death
i first saw it dingy new york in 1967
when i stood on horseback before it
but turned away because i didn't know enough math
the same orthographic storm redeemed
by illusions of immortality
now it was redeemed by nothing
it just was   i remembered also the poem i wrote:
never say
it says
it talks
it speaks
because it
does not
back then the cleaving of language from world
was a welcome and healing discovery
now it was the wailing wind of a disaster
what did i do for a lifetime

a wave of compassion for my mother seized me
her courage was greater than mine
she had made irrevocable decisions
her imagination more serious than mine
she made worlds that had to be
lived in by everyone
who came near hers

i am the regrets she dragged around

for the nurses

the inventor of heaven and hell was clever
thank you dante for slicing them into circles
and placing purgatory between them
try to get away from those three   good luck
you'll end up even worse   on a billboard or in
the mouth of a politician or a salesman spraying
words with poison from within
my advice is: be nice   to yourself and others
there is nothing to it   and get the right pills
anyone who keeps your pills from you will go to hell
to one of its deeper circles   one that will nonetheless
feel as gentle as rain
but anyone who keeps pills from the old and frail
that one will go to hell's worst deepest pit of pain

who's right

a fan wrote to me: i think
that you and your mother are indissoluble
i fought against that thought
surely i hadn't done two years of furious
(or not) analysis on my aborning self
to sever myself from her   and in the process
created a myriad of selves   a starry sky
i had even acquired irony (at basement-level prices
in the fin-de-siècle-just-upchucked)
an irony in the dedication to my first memoir
"to mother, of course"
i had won that "of course" the hard way:
it took a lot of reading and a lot of fucking people
of the 20th century to keep that "of course" alive
other dependencies and surrogates had their way with me
and my speech writing and living in that fight
in the end I have this thought: my fan was right
the fans are always right   my own pretensions not so much

UPLIFT

Uplift

you're stuck on a desert island and you have no memory
but you have a pen and a stack of dry
banana leaves   your writer's block is suddenly gone
you're on to new poem   no ship to the rescue

what pleasure to quit scanning for it!

it's like the joy of once finding that english
no longer had a second person plural!
everyone was me then! everyone i called "you"
was one of a kind that was also me
or close enough

where i was born the plural was scary
every single person i addressed
had an army   and every adult did
even your mother and the guy called father

strangers had so many armies
they shot you in your dreams from passing trucks

when i crossed the atlantic ocean
i got away from the second person plural
to delight in fearless address
i stood up like whitman on a mound of corpses
and glimpsed the brilliant future

of my new country   and i lived in it!

but lately in the future
people stopped using the personal "you"
and are addressing themselves to everyone at once
with a collective pronoun through ubiquitous screens

an ocean of "we" flooded the world

but i am still me

this last ocean i crossed has no name
no ship will ever head for my particular island
i don't contain multitudes
i lost the useful wisdom you once said i had
i don't know from distance
i have no idea what time it is where you are

if you are sometime startled awake it's not the phone
or the alarm of the i-something machine
it's this poem mouthing to itself the odd fact
of this new ocean
between a stranded i and a lost you

this job saw better days

to the previous questions i answered:
the job is to enliven: you can do this by making more life
making others horny enough to make life
refusing to be bored and doing something about it
making people laugh cry scream pee come
or being so magnetic everybody's prostheses fly to the stage.
Except for such effects, poets are useless.
Surviving at all cost is not an accomplishment.
"All cost" is too expensive. "Me" is a tool.
I'll just keep going South where people get crazier
and shabbier, and a sober god is rarer than snow.
I'll trade my goods for ease insomnia and abandon.

I did. I have my doubts now.

ah, ach, vai bilingvism

From what language do you begin to drive your sentence?
In what direction?
Which way do you translate?
From your native tongue to your childhood
or from the new to think yourself into the world
that is your home now?

In what language do you dream?
I don't dream in language. I dream in pictures.
Sometimes people from long ago
who spoke in my old language
appear in my dreams. Are they from there
or from here where I dream them?
In my dreams I sometimes read in a language
I never spoke or read but I'm dream-fluent in.
No one speaks in any language in my dreams
yet there it is, written and spoken by someone
I forgot already when I wake up.
I have no idea what that gibberish is on the tape.
You shouldn'ta done all that dreaming, girl.
Does here start there or here?
Is it arabic or sanskrit and is there still
a calendar on the wall gregorian or hebrew
that isn't about time   a calendar of stories.
The place you are what once you were is there
lost in one of those nonsense tales
that was somehow both home and elsewhere.
And where are they now who knew you there?
When you travel between languages what suit
do you wear, what suitcase do you carry?

the new golden wretched

Google-worthy immigrants are to be found
say the fat natives wrapped in fur & fear
in the 1938-1948 wave and the post-commie
era 1989-2001 when politics was clear

after that as Gogol Bordello sings
"we are coming rougher"

we walk on desert rocks   come out of tunnels
we left our kin in a storm of shards
barrel bombs that tore up legs eyes arms hair
a rain of meat that we once called "love"

now mud air mushrooms roots grubs

those refugees of two decades ago
who came under the umbrella of idealism
by boat and plane and real politik
do not want us   they have forgotten

"we come rougher"
unwanted   parcelled out like fuel for the engines
of power's calculated mercy
but "rough" is just another texture of despair
whether it's 1941, 2015 or sometime imminent and new

history doesn't take vacations
it only stops to take a breath to change
bibs continents and menus before it eats again

to a young poet

the trick is not being misunderstood
everybody is
but to be misunderstood by someone who matters
as in "oh you won't believe who misunderstands me now!"

but who that someone is is hard to say
it isn't all cream and peaches as you know
from all the screens and books
you still have to work to love someone
and harder yet to have them love you back

there are no short walks there are no safe objects
the fear of art and the price of art walk hand in hand
on a street papered with theory
your professors have mistaken you for their wallet

Putin statue project

for Nadezhda Mandelstam and Pussy Riot

Working class you don't exist any more.
Stalin saw to it that you died on your shovels
after digging graves for poets who committed suicide.
Their mothers wrote diaries with piss in snow
while felling trees without gloves at twenty below
and one of them lived to write a book. That was long ago.
Now take your nostalgia to the mall, but don't relax.
There is something about Russia. In the early 60s
I loved my Russian teacher's miniskirt, a boy-lust carousel.
She liked to wheel about until I hurt and spun in a red daze
lost in her skirt, a wind-whipped sail. I wanted communism!
Putin your predecessors did much so you can now nuke for kicks.
So what if next morning you'll be sober and we'll be dead?
I'll sail with a miniskirt!
And you'll be that mass of rocks looming ahead.

patria

To us it's a house of mirrors.
To them a glass house.
You wonder why they throw stones?

Frying Pan from the Flea Market

a thing means nothing
if it isn't used and shared
this pan was used many times
the stew in it eaten by many

people aged as slices of the past
surfaced with foods they no longer ate

the pan itself returned to earth

the servant turned tyrant knows
power is worth nothing in itself
until it shares itself with the people it oppresses

to be a thing means nothing by itself
the thing says as soon as it is made

the surprise

we live in a practical world
there are facts
they are understood
if they are not they can be explained
it doesn't take long

after the facts are established
and the world of sense agreed on
how does one fill the coldness of space
the immensity of time

by thinking up worlds that are not like the world of sense
by defending that which is powerless to become fact
living stories that make their own sense
their space of self-understood unfolding
of dream laundry

laughter is the release from sense
but look! surprise! it's a child! how unexpected!

who ever expects a child? (even if they call it that)
this child is the world of sense meeting the world of nonsense

the edges where they rub together are incompatible
but laughter has released them from war

"The Gordian Knot"
what kind of name is that for a child?

The Gordian Knot came into the world to make sense of it

the gordian knot the paradox
only laughter can cut

this is the world with clowns I hope
the unborn babe said

You should never speak
    ill of the dead
  you've never read
      *

Encyclopedist—one who rides a cyclops (Laura)
      *

Painted Town
    Tough Titty
      *

We were working on the derangement of all the senses, but now we are working
on the re-arrangement of some of them, the ones we still possess
      *

To my pedicurist: with each step I take toward war I'll remember your hands
      *

I blame it on my dignity
      *

You're a stripper, you are never very far from the mind of God
      *

For success you have to fight against your own reputation
      *

Why do TV anchors stand up now? It's painful.
      *

"...this time however I come as the victorious Dionysus, will turn the world into
a holiday...Not that I have much time..."
      *

Will we ever be safe from the dramatic monologue?
      *

Post cogitationem, omnia animalia tristia sunt but consolation comes when my
keyboard leaves out letters: typing "ex" for instance, when I meant to type "sex."
Enchanted, no longer annoyed, I thank you flawed mechanism for putting a
smile in my cogitum
      *

Persimmon, you are Rimbaud

family matters

i turned prudes into nymphomaniacs
and nymphomaniacs into prudes
what kind of talent is that?

living they called it in those days
when ancient words circulated like old money
with zeroes not yet sliced off

i noticed that long after the zeroes were gone
the common folk still called them millions
they were loathe to let go of the denomination
that made them feel rich during inflation

the five hundred million note featuring tesla
during the nation of milovan radović
now rests in a frame on my bookcase of terror-fiction
a domestic region of unstoppable friction

the birth of panic

The delight-suffused nymph ambushed by Pan in the afternoon
composed her speech all the way from the grotto with the spring
to the crenellated tower where dwelt a cuirassed father, a husband,
and a corsetted mother. Her dishevelled description horrified them
as she knew it would: hoofs, hair everywhere, even in the ears,
coarse goat-thighs similar to deer bones, the reward of hunting dogs.
On the object of humiliation she swore she did not gaze
for fear of dying from esthetic shock (a bit too dainty, thought
the audience) even as she went on with the long nose capped by eyes
filled with dreadful knowledge of a sort she dared not imagine,
and into whose black deeps she did not gaze, and the obsidian-red lips
that were an imitation of stone, but were in fact fleshy and lurid.
All this "ick" she added to Pan hoping to squelch the delight seeping
through her pores in amber beads of sweat as fragrant as goat cheese.
Her ick had the intended effect, but her father suggested removing the "k,"
too noble a letter to allow a creature that loathsome to the gold cross
graved on his chest armor he traced for emphasis, watching the husband
who was more circumspect, his expected jealous rage hampered
by an involuntary erection that pressed into the steel of his mail codpiece.
The power of Pan to project desire even through the medium of his wife
was barely held in check by her "ick," or "ic," as his father-in-law would
have it. This took place in 1352 or 2016, let's say, just before a crusade,
and it was truly the birth of "panic," a modern feeling that replaced,
or took its place along the ancient father Fear and that of his son, Terror.
Pan, squeezed by vineyards and walls, turned on the TV in his hidden grotto.
This crusade, the corsetted mother said, should rid the world of Pan forever.
When you men return victorious we will build a shining city over
the forested hill and the monster's cave, so hasten to Jerusalem!
And you, young wench, show me where Pan suffused you, she cried,
with genuine Panic, fearing neither father Fear nor son Terror.

confusing job

So we are bad because we have parents and ideas?
Like most people we try to say what the dead tell us
to say and pass on the message unchanged until
we become the dead ourselves
and then it's our turn to pass on to the living
what the previous dead passed on to us.
The dead talk to each other in another way
but only poets can hear them speak that way.
And then there is trouble. Language revolts.
Words get emancipated, changed, people refuse to die.
Really, everything I said just now is gibberish
but it's too late: the dead heard me and said: "you just wait!"
Poets are the worst. Like old static radios they sow dissent.

grow up

You don't die when you've had enough of life
you die when life's had enough of you.
A healer in the business of keeping life liking you
makes a lot of house calls to the singular "you,"
a unique product of two billion years of evolution.
It is both heavy and amusing that the vast universe
has come up with you, a goof, in the business
of entertaining dark thoughts for an uneasy audience.
That's the amusing part. The heavy part is that
you have anything to say about it, and you do.

art for art's sake

the hive is overfilled
with meaning we put in
to make it live

if it lives
it is the twin of the world
the dead fill with meaning
to keep it dead

other twin worlds birthed them

we meaning-stuffers live or dead
are worker bees but rarely fed

dead yet frustrated

Why do the dead need us at all?
Because they don't have throats
and their genitals no longer host seeds or eggs.
So we do the job of being media
for their words and spooge.
The dead reproduce in two ways:
through the end of the living
and through poetry.
This is why there are more of them than us:
each of us plus every word we speak
is made a citizen in the Land of the Dead.
In the Land of the Dead there are two kinds of beings:
people like us, who died, and words
which are used to communicate between us and them,
words are the pets of the dead, messenger pigeons.
Only faster. The Land of the Dead is orderly.
They seek poets in particular for our words.
They nicknamed us Stooges of Los Muertos.
Our job is to be their typewriters.
They like to be heard, they type on us hard when we sleep.
Most of them died before the internet, they pound the keys
of Underwoods and Royals loud and fast. Those orgasms
are neither spontaneous nor dreams. They are the typing
of the dead, both-sides-of-Hades orgasms.
But we are bad. Awake or not we are all
like the next-to-the-last person in the game of "telephone"
who whispers a totally off-the-wall phrase into the next ear.
And when the last ear-person speaks it out loud
everyone alive's convulsed by laughter.
This play was easy once, a whim of flighty Eros.
Now you must leave your cell-phones at the door
and have no fear of germs when your lips touch another's ear.
Why are we so bad? Must be we don't want to be dead.

gemini

(from the paleo-diet)

two eyes for looking
two eyes for seeing

two ears for listening
two ears for hearing

two sexes for reproduction
two sexes for pleasure

two hands for everything
two brains for two hands

cooperation is not optional
not available by request

cannot be ignored for difficulty
it is always in practice

all visible organs equipped
to do the job of the mouth

only a full body strike
by the invisible organs

introduces one to another
and to the mouth they serve

last words

Dying poets don't make speeches.
We utter a final burst of words
that may be an imprecation at what we see coming,
an unpunctuated unspaced string of perfect (non)sense.

Anselm said "damiunalta!" which might mean
"give me another!" in one of the many languages he knew.
Another body, or another chance, or just another shot of morphine.
Articulated last words are posthumous inventions.
Goethe's "Mehr Licht" was neither "More Enlightenment!"
nor "Open the curtains!" but "mehrlicht" prophesizing Metternich.
The last words of poets are particularly prized by fearful readers.
They are thought to be pithy summations, supremely instructional.
The last words of poets may be aphoristic conclusions
of decades spent discovering and understanding them.
In the future people will no longer have time for poetry
but won't mind the abbreviated form, the last Cliff note.
The truth is that poets like all humans
die saying the same thing emphasized in two different ways:
"What was THAT? and "What WAS that?"
I'm from both schools. Poetry is both the thing
and what the thing does. Some poets when expiring
oblige the future by not returning to correct fabrications.
Everyone will find out soon enough.
And yet I bow to the common belief:
poetry is the art of last words.
If spoken posthumously or not does not matter.
Whatever awe still attaches to the obscurity of our verse
is OK with me. I approve of the grave conceit
that we speak the truth with our last breath.
What no one needs to know is that dying poets
just like their readers speak the truth *only* with their last breath.
We rightly fear our last outpouring of wisdom because it

may be common, the animal's last cry, articulated only
if we are lucky. To readers it is their own wisdom avant-spoken.
When a poet truly dies, reader, there is no time
to waste talking, so we must all train for this together.

la chose

there is no "free speech"
everything you say will be held against you.
especially or only if it's true.
meaning it is a thing that isn't words.

using words to enter thingness
is not possible says the thing
in not so many words.

a story is a thing the storyteller's
tellings change as if something happened.
what happens cannot be told.
it is too busy being the untold thing.

stories are from a place that projects
things passing for history masked in lessons,
passing through the isness of things
looking for the verb that shatters them.

no se puede vivir sin amar (lorca)

movies are much sadder than life
life hurts more
and lasts longer

unable to give or receive
love to or from those nearest
the poet gave and received
it to and from all strangers

died from what remained
untouched at his fingertips

mission impossible

i was raised by communists with ink in their blood and blood in their ink
i was a child of lead
i had quick hands and awe of the heroic dead
the dust devils i inhaled were famous writers
i was once a child
books drove me wild
from hermanstadt to kolosvar
rome paris new york baltimore and boston
i sought books to read for instruction and language
i clerked for some of the greatest bookstores
and in turn i wrote the best i could about what was my life:
old books and girls with glasses.
i had two jobs, two vocations, and three failures:
the jobs were professor and reporter.
the vocations: poet and pleasing women.
my vocations lent credibility to my jobs
which made me a pretty good living.
i sounded like i knew what i was talking about
and the labor spent elaborating my ignorance
served my vocations.
i was busy.
and the failures:
i was not a very good husband father or driver

it's not yours to forget

u can only forget what's yours to forget
u can't forget what i remember
even if u were there and your name is
Notoriously Reliable

u can't seriously remember
what i am trying to forget
forgetting is art not witness prose

what i want to forget
i must first remember
so that i can disremember

for what u remember
there is no remedy in art

the brain will forget for us
but i want to forget before
nature or witnesses do it for me

the art of forgetting
the thing cannot be saved from erasure
but can be forgotten on purpose and in style

the art of forgetting
borders the shore of oblivion
but keeps from crossing over
it must remember itself first to take form

a lifetime of living
half of which which was dedicated
to forgetting must be art

to be successful in what we call life
we must practice the art of forgetting
so that we might reach the next

of those things best recalled before dark
of a nature that makes them unforgettable
things that aren't yours to forget

persons in midst of events
objects in the midst of persons

they are of such importance
they cannot be surrendered to nature
before being dealt with by art

if it's the last thing i do
i must forget u
i must forget u

the retrovisionary

for jeff miller

in his living room a tv that only plays news from the 1950s 60s
and 1970s when he wrote his visionary poetry
for the 21st century he didn't live to see

now on the streets outside
gender-neutral youth clad in leggings
printed with his retrovisionary poetry
animated by their walking or dancing
are wondering what news could have
been news before they were born

jeff never made the news but he was and is news
he made and makes it by having moved in time
to his own dance which is also theirs

our corpse mistress

for andrea garland

the letter on her flesh did not
vacate the alphabet as you then thought.
you were privileged to be the first to see
the new ring when she was young.

seeing her regal head brought later on a spike
did not inhibit you: you still knew her.
the courier said: reanimate her if you like.
but she was still alive and her ring shone hidden.

how many times can you be reborn?
as many as you like if you possess the ring.
the trick is to show it while it still burns
to someone proud to be the first to see it

someone who honored by her knowing
will recall it in its glory when her severed head
is brought before him by a cruel enemy.

our best self always has a shot at that far border
provided that a great someone honors the primacy
of your textual self not yet capable of knowing
its own integrity before it knows its orders.

this will not be recorded
it is a love letter

the enemy is the tedium
the tedium is the medium
a dullard's nonamiability
nothing but banality
he wears company down to a nub

a human pencil doomed to irritate
the future that will now remove
his vocal chords
to make no more words
his letters flee the keyboard

the i writing this will never be that dullard
the he writing this was chosen by the imp
of her artist youth brimming with courage
to feature timelessness while there is time

Utopia is Everywhere

Cyberspace is just more space
as more and more people crowd the planet.
It makes Malthus at once wrong again.
If you can stand or lie on one square foot
inside a vast mental empire in the company
of all your friends, even the ones unmet,
what need have you of space?
You're working every second of your life,
fulfilling work, painless, pleasurable,
even musical, communal, fed by molecules at hand.
Virtuality is communism realized at last.
What's "reality" anyway?
Just another virtuality, plus pain.

the internet

if all your senses are occupied
God will have no place to sit

if all your circuits are busy
the unknown can't reach you

mystery doesn't like call-waiting
it hangs up and calls someone else

you must always keep a line open
despite your job in the glass prison

your full-time job in the glass prison
building layers in the glass prison

using your imagination of freedom
to perfect the transparency of glass

the end of your polishing job
is the end of your imagination

you see your chained insect legs
for a second before you expire

greater transparency no leg room
the flight attendant apologizes

there is transparency in the hive
all but your once-self is visible

to time:

the secret goes both ways:
you're not the only one gets to eat my brain.
I can also eat yours. So put away the spoon.

one topos

"Breasts: there is something / between us." Larry Fagin

there *was* something between us
but the thing that stood between us
wasn't breasts   it was psychology
pills got rid of it   but just like breasts
psyche too hovered briefly
before it vanished to live in novels

the trinity of discontinued lines:
breasts   feelings   novels

my ears stand like a bat's at sunset
listening for the one mosquito
that survived the poisoned air
when our story flew the coop for fiction

nature used to defend itself through redundancy
but it could in the end only make so many copies
and only seasonally at that

but breasts and sentiments in books
are never tired of full narrative drag
they reproduce in infinite mirrored closets
of language the wordless something
the once-between-us glyph of the thing
that said "I" all the time and then apologised for it

Ah vampires refreshed in the dead internets of one minute ago
you can't fool this attentive bat
watching for that lone mosquito
in the only place to view the topos from:

the place of oneself alone without an other
to fake with words that in-between.

Time pays geography a high price for her contours,
it extorts an even higher price for drawing borders.

in the winter of our discontent

She thinks that I am everything that's wrong with her
& that if I go away everything that's wrong with her will
go away, too. She knows that what was wrong was there
before me, and that it was this that drew me to her.
If I take it with me now only the good part will remain.
What that is she doesn't quite know yet. I certainly don't.
I'm not sorry that I loved her. Maybe that was the bad part
and she hated me for it. I was no angel either.

new season

spring is here! the bats are awake!

are there any holy sites like Jerusalem
on the internet
something we can really fight about?

nature is so exuberant!

my iphone can barely take it it's gone batty
after i lost and found it in the grass
i manually decapitated it
for automatically capitalising
every first letter in a sentence

let's not speak of this   i'll try not to
let's just look up at the clouds
where the poem before this one

snatched a last mosquito like a bat
a hawk snatched the bat
the verdant hill is in a john donne mood
even some capitals seem ok far away

world full

there are now more ways of writing
than there is anything to write about

meaningless text need not exist
meaning is fundamental
to the fundamentalists erasing it

in order to be erased
a text must first exist
then it must mean something
to those who think it worth erasing

they must be young these furiosos
to swarm so eagerly between
flapping sheets of newsprint

our best hope now is to forget that folly
text is inflated and unstable
the only stable currency is youth
print is no longer common currency

in the old texts lie wholly conquered languages
even their silence now fails to bring up
what the point was in the first place
what was it that was worth fighting for

it's time to erase the overemphatic past
its fervent shapes intentions emissaries and mercenaries
and the words in which it revealed its violence

going there now is like finding love in a threesome
one found it but one can't remember who won

none of the participants care much for it either
and if there were words for it then there aren't any now
the black & white sun of the page annihilated sentiment

reality-shows talking heads and projections
of young bodies have even downgraded
the last pleasure of ordinariness:
the right to be trivial in our own world

advent of the parahuman

as in paramilitary
not the posthuman who was half-machine
but a posthuman indentured to the machine
in exchange for staying half-human

the parahuman works outside the machine
which has become smart enough
to overcome itself by employing
its unpredictable human half
to teach itself unpredictability

the parahuman is a mercenary
fighting for the enemy in exchange
for being allowed to be the enemy

persona

When the persona wears thin, the self emerges.
Eegads, it's a monster! A second placenta! It grows
to defend the monster of self within it
until the monster is born. Egg ads, a new human!

in the fold

until everyone lives in the future
a great many will keep living in the past

yesterday's faithful lie about the yard
like broken machines in the spring

and as the survivors die off
the past loses its power accordingly:
its technology dies with the users,
its memory dies with its archives

if there are signals beyond silence
they are not human they are other
organisms communicating their
own urgencies to their new spawn

on the bright glass polished by us

was the future something worth dying for
when the only idea worth dying for
will be getting away from people
who have ideas worth your dying for?

pastoral

i live in the woods   i have no change in my pockets
i never jingle coins
the extortion machine called city
peddles sugar and turns big bills into small coins
i have no change in the woods where change
is a constant i'm too slow to know

i'm the Jingler of Unseen Change
on the next hill over lives the Keeper of Rhythm
and the Drummer whose beats are in my heart
one is a boy one is a deer and the third is an oak

the Collector has no fixed address
but when he shows up you better lay down that axe
address him as *Señor* Death
he comes for the Tree Tax

palo duro, blanco canyon, apacheria, texas 2014

please distribute these rifles to the audience
to mark the anniversary october 31 1871
when u.s. troops under general mackenzie began
the eradication of indians here
at the count of three put barrels under your chin
and listen without moving to a one-hour lecture
covering two hundred years of dirt oil aliens and space
and the correlatives of money and poetry accumulated
or spent in the resulting surpluses

(spends forty minutes here detailing history)

a dollar is a dollar if it buys a rose or a bullet
poetry is the fingerprint each individual leaves on the dollar
each poem is a person who leaves dna on paper

my modest proposal is to eliminate money
and trade one another for the goods we produce
individually or in small bands
poetry is the currency of the future
or what goes on between you and me

ozark sonnet

i like to live where (human) sensibilities are still
shockable though nature sees to its own business
adding winter stash to its wank tank its jack sack
jack please take that to the bank keep the change
only a pine tree can teach you what a pine tree is (basho)
but any particular pine tree has an encrypted password
that depends on what it is you want to know from it
every degree of curiosity requires an equivalent hard skin
from the writer who thinks herm want to know
and is tough enough to go on when the pine asks
what are humans for. the obvious answer (to the pine) is
this book is made from pine. that's me. so take back
your questions people   words are cysts give back my sap
philosophers are fascists looking for cheap coffins

cedar top goddesses from phil's sawmill

The cedar goddesses lie down on saw-horses
debarked by rain smooth like movie stars
sinuous knotty tops sloped with open eyes
we lock gazes forged in what I'd like to think
is inter-regnum lust but is only my artsy awe.
The sawmiller's wife was just about to toss them to the fire.
They weren't good enough for lumber. Their fragile skin
accomodated no smoothing tool. She gave them to us
gladly moments before tossing them into the pyre.
They should make me a fine arbor for sitting in to think.
Is art worth saving anything from fire?
Or they'll frame another something no less tragic.
Maybe I'll ice the pond and slide on them, let's say,
a woodophile atop those eyes that do not look away.

a tenth of a second in oz

andrei: watcha doin?
laura: darning moth holes.
andrei: what an eighteenth century woman would do.
laura: right.
andrei: but she wouldn't be watching her iPad.
laura: no. she wouldn't.

*evening feb 16 coming from the shop through snow after i made a fire in there so the
sterile-water jugs for my electric Bad Boy wouldn't freeze*

i read books not people

to my rural fellows

these people are smart
they can read you really fast
but they get stupid quick
when they stick to their reading
as the next "you" shows up in
a new york minute followed
by another "you" and another
and by the time a country minute
(which is five years) has gone by
the "you" they first knew is back
now they feel smug but a bit abashed
they suspect something happened
maybe they are not such fast readers
then they machete the snake of doubt
you can meet their expectations now
after they do the snake chopping
they'll never know what they expected
he's a mystery they say chop chop
of course I am to you but the snake knew
and can't tell   you chopped him all up

love sonnet to aliens

The known universe is self-referential: it has no choice.
unknown universes can see us and smell us
we hope that they have a sense of humor about it.
I want to learn at the knee and suck at the tit
of a totally unknown universe composed of wit.
When I smell a rusted clamp or a newly greased vice
or a warm horse with a rising yen for a mare
I think I'm closing in on a universe alien and near.
I hope it thinks me tragic and funny on the cusp
of the back-kick the warm horse owes his honey.
What seems self-referential is just aliens going to dinner
to watch aliens. Cylons with nylons draw lots
for this perfumer-in-training wearing his old boy hots.

eating you up

my writing will always be smart and sexy
even if I won't
though it's hard to imagine now
when I'm ingesting your attributes
ingesting not "digesting" you heard me right
cannibal confessions are hard to come by
in written form except for a tobias schneebaum
here and there cannibals are for the most part
not eager to write their memoirs
but I may just be old-fashioned
these days cannibalism writes itself
the alphabet of taste takes dictation

in the sheep meadow

for stanley moss

the meanderings of a mind that refuses to accept
what it knows is only a neuron in a sheepskin vest
refuses to accept what it knows so running suits it
it doesn't care whether knowledge was implanted
or gone as long as the sheepskin keeps him warm

orpheus wore his sheepskin from may until december
for milennia: the only sign of him was a trace of scent
from his lyre as he wandered alone from thrace
to studios in los angeles where he was rarely sent

sometimes he exchanged his lyre for a mike stand
to work a crowd that captured him with a lover's lies
in a pinch he could sing esperanto and fill a room with sighs
a nerve in his pitch-dark memory kept a dimly lit map
to the boneyard with the better graves on the other side

yet he allowed nothing but love to swap his sheepskin
for a black and white tux of an evening on the town
and that's a stubborn streak that all poets must keep
a silver string a wandering eye a vow to joy a sheep

Questions

for Lisa C.

The quality of questions gives you a glow, Curiosity!
They have improved and so have you since spouses
laid down the line, "If you can Google it don't ask me."
The horrors of history, the schisms, the ripped blouses
have stepped to the forefront of the Great Wall of info,
or so it seemed at first when facts called themselves Data.
Then Data became questionable like the language it was
made of and a shadow Google rose behind the eyebrows
of baffled satyrs, awkward nymphs, dancers and dunces
asking questions that even Pinterest couldn't answer.
Did daddy use his grave to make me write a poem? Did
that raised arm with its glistening sweat circle
just become an aura over my slightly worried head?
Next time I'm in San Francisco I'll ask you these in bed.

bonhomie

for pat nolan

one day I decided to go to work
at the la vie en rose café
the place smelled like sun lotion
and the locals were taking coffee
with cream lots of cream it was
an endurance contest until noon
in other corners reports and poems
were also being filed but mostly
legs were being crossed and recrossed
newspapers were self-importantly
creased and items torn out for later
and menus were being read with great
concentration some accents were heard
australian and english i believe
the news was dire the menu had not
changed in years the flies were happy

a scarf for the tropics

is what the girl on the barstool at molly's
was knitting with two huge wooden needles
and I mean huge like walking sticks or lances
she hooked that fabric roughly leaving holes
for wind rainstorms and all the people in new orleans
lady I cried out is that gargantua's christmas present
a scarf for the tropics
you got that right buddy she said I'm the next storm

(for SuZi)

tu fu

vices of the city
defects of character
one nature

the idiot at the front desk

why do you think I'm at the front desk?
the tattoo'd genius they've got in the back
and buried right under *his* feet is god
they have a technique these guys
they believe in the meritocracy of the first impression.
the most beautiful woman in the village
draws spectators not just customers
spectators are future customers who feed
on her looks to make themselves richer
to be worthy of her to make her surrender
and when she does they close their eyes
and when they open them they are holding the genius
from the back in their arms and he speaks with an accent.
god squirms under the ground and a new consuming class
is born to his squirming delight
out of which he fashions a slew of new front desk idiots.
and so does beauty spread skin deep in offices and on screens

PRIVATE UTOPIA

private utopia

for eva leonte

a tropical bum is buffeted by the wind and rain in stockholm
but he is not deported he is loved instead and given a warm room
and celebrated in an elegant mansion by civilized and witty people
in a mansion where the machinery of the universe has gone in reverse

from: dan shafran's guide to eminent vagabonds and exiles in sweden: rené descartes and lenin

rené descartes

an icy day in stockholm   even the locals say so
dan takes me to a graveyard surrounding an old church
and points to the frigid granite profile above the door

rené descartes
  in trouble with the pope
    in trouble with the dutch
       having gotten a servant girl in trouble in amsterdam
      his daughter francine dead of scarlet fever
        in trouble with pascal who accused him of getting rid of god

migrating from one teaching gig to another
        nassau bavaria paris dordrecht
never without admirers
among them queen elisabeth of bohemia
to whom he dedicated principia philosophiae in french in 1647

rené vagabonds with his pen always moving
  a step ahead of the inquisition that had gotten galileo
in the hope of a permanent roof over his head & a subsidy

at last he finally finds the right queen praise philosophia!
he is hired to tutor queen christina of sweden
a real job with health benefits freedom to speculate and a future
      she may at last be the right royal!

if she was rené never found out
shortly after arrival on an icy day in stockholm
he takes his philosopher's walk toward his pupil's palace
for her first lesson   collapses

and dies of pneumonia
not because of the bone-chilling wind
but because of the protestant queen's insistence that he rise
early for her lessons

rené descartes was not a morning person

after he died he was interred in a graveyard used for unbaptised infants
  because he was a catholic in a protestant country

after he was thus reposed queen christina abdicates her throne
  and converts to roman catholicism

but she'd have done better to sleep late and learn in the afternoon
        it was her schedule not god
            that killed descartes

his books were already blackindexed by the church
  and as pascal noted rené wasn't much for god

nor did the french let him rest long
   they moved his remains (on an icy day)
     intending to bury him in the pantheon
        but as he waits for the paperwork
he's parked between two monks in the abbey of st. germain-des-prés

and because my teeth were chattering
  from the baltic sea wind of march 2013
    one hundred years and one month since the author
      of "passions of the soul" died of pedagogy
        and interred in the waiting room of la gloire
          where he still waits   a bohemian vagabond to the end

dan and i walk inside the church whose graveyard also briefly hosted him
   and the ushers wave us gracefully in
just as a chorus of beautiful young swedes
     soar unto the glorious finale of bach's magnificat
      to a great standing ovation and loud applause

they are not applauding for you
  dan said
i know that   they are applauding rené descartes

lenin

after 20 hours of flying
   before i even checked into my hotel
      dan had me driven from the airport
         straight to the royal library in stockholm
            where he works
he led me past carrels filled with silent scholars
   to a plain wooden table in a bare small room
it was the table where lenin-in-swedish-exile worked
   having signed himself in the register of 1909
      as j. frey
         and as ulyanov in 1910

when i stretched my hands over the plain oak surface
   polished by the hands and shirtsleeves
      of the founder of the soviets
         his resonant voice came booming into my brain
            with the command to now visit
               all the libraries of his many exiles
                  and write a poem in each of them

and since i was now in his second
      the first having been the british museum library
         where he had signed in as richter
            i owed him a poem immediately

lenin boomed with rhetorical intransigence
      that having read my poem about his british library stint
(it is well known that ghosts read all about themselves)
            he had now instructed dan shafran
               (in the same booming metempsychotic fashion)
to hand me a folder of documents about his well-documented
            exiles to sweden
               which dan did
well-documented indeed

were the houses he'd lived in
  no longer there
but photographed just before being demolished
    there were others
      never photographed
        that had become mythical in stockholm
lenin had slept everywhere in stockholm
    in the swedish version of "washington slept here"
(though it is known that he rarely slept and always studied)
      thus
concluded the booming lenin voice in my brain
    you must now go to zurich
      to the library of my other bitter exiles
        and write another poem

i tore my hot itching hands away from the mediumatic table
    terrified of the enormous task before me
      after 20 hours of flight

i had the brief thought that his ghost always chose mediums for this job
        among exiles from his utopia
        people like dan and me
        who had barely escaped the thoughts
        born in him in this library

we exiles always carry photographs of those thoughts
    in our minds
        even long after the utopia was demolished
lenin still the iconic figure of our youth
    broadcasting well to us
      in the socialist kingdom of sweden
        (not far from russia)
but i became truly sad
when dan told me that soviet tourists in the 20th century
    each with a flower in his hand
      waited in long lines for many hours

to lay this flower on lenin's oak desk
  having traveled for days by bus direct from the kremlin
  where they had laid more flowers on his glass tomb

this was their reward for being heroes of labor

and so with hands calloused by steel and shovel
  they tenderly laid their grateful gift
    on the worktable of the great dead comrade
      for whom they had become labor heroes
        and spent long nights on hard snowy roads

        cupping a tender flower

and here i was
  with my bourgeois complaint
    20 hours in flight

what is that to a century of dead tired subjects of a library scholar?

ok said dan
    this is the 21st century
      you can go to your hotel to sleep now
        there is always time for a poem

march 15, 2013 stockholm

87

time with swedish motif

the original one
  swans in the frozen baltic
    not moving a polished feather
      gustav pointing snowy sword to russia
        he lost the swedish empire to it
the bronze body of a great actress
            in front of the stockholm lyric theatre
              cuddles a sleeping drunk
                she's heated from within
a castle made of ice in Umea
  a translator slides down the steep tower
    he makes untranslatable sound at bottom
on an ice bench viking lovers
  look up to listen then resume kissing

minneapolis
  rain mixed with snow
    towers combined for heat with glass bridges
      book readers warm in the modern library theater
        we make ice castles all winter a local tells me
and just like in the first sweden "going north" means dying

ikea's swedish meatballs
  are mired in scandal
    "horsemeat found in beef and reindeer!"
      horsemeat from romania
        comments swedish food inspector
          "revenge for EU rules on killing pigs with needle
            instead of tradition-bound knife and rope"

yes
  two climates
    three meats

one tit for tat
  much snow and ice
  prized heat

when young I followed spring from city to city
  fleeing south to north
    now I stumble through winter south to north
    one life one meat one tat for tit

my ancient people of the tongue

for ruxandra cesereanu

Wanderer, lover of fresh summer fruit, mushrooms, leaves
I bring good news from Transylvania, city of Cluj:
under baroque arcs in narrow alleys under gargoyled eaves
you'll find Café Bulgakov, a stone maze of vaulted cellars,
named after the author of *The Master and Margarita*,
a novel where the devil is a gourmand who takes a soul
with only the best wine and condimented hors-de-hell-oeuvres.
At Café Bulgakov the menu is almost as thick as the novel,
its first five chapters listing dishes such as "Wolfram's Chicken,"
"Flight of the Demon Quail Wings," and "Margarita's Braised Ribs Hovel,"
followed by numerous chapters of Romanian, Hungarian, nomad
creations, tested by history in tents and palaces, on horseback
or seated before stone castle fireplaces in fierce winters:
Sarmalutze, Mushroom Paprikash, Perishoare, Ficat cu Knigle
mixes of ground meats with the morning's mushrooms, cherries,
sweet and sour, melded with cumin, fresh basil, green onion,
paprika, drak, and mysterious other herbs present before Columbus
brought corn, potatoes, yams, and sugar from the New World.
Punctuated like a long, dark sentence by bitter or light beers,
wines of honeyed hues, reddish sunsets, black centuries of song,
I relished shameless in my childhood's lost flavors.
My birthplace and its many mouths of feasts and hunger on my tongue.

June 2014, Cluj, Romania

kenny's deli

(from his own words in 2014)

Kenny smart Jew born in Queens is taken every birthday
until the age of ten to his father's deli pickles and hallah
enough for all Eastern-European jews 1888-1989.
Kenny leaves New York for the best French cooking school,
advances layer by layer through the Cold War and the Fall
of the Berlin Wall when he returns from Europe an accomplished
rouladeur a shiny monocled, tower-of-babel-tall pastry chef
festooned with two china-silk blue ribbons pinned to his chest,
his fingers at Chez Kenward roll minuscule roe over grains of rice
on top of a crisp leaf so tender it sears only under his eyes,
an arch of his eyebrow enough to topple sous-chefs into hell.
He brings the caviared rice to the center of the bumpy sèvres
plate with surgical precision signed "made by Kenward
wearing a blindfold while squirting fig syrup that forms
sometimes an aleph sometimes a mayan glyph or a cuneiform
that circumnavigates riced caviar with beatific grace," words
swallowed before read and then drowned in Chateau-Neuf.
The fate of all poetry, sighs Kenny. It was original, too.
A quartet in formal dress moonlights from an alcove above
for Kenny who carries a diamond for Estelle in a beribboned box
one tenth of his family fortune that by May if the market
stays at current levels will appreciate to what few imagine

but in October it collapses this market and the long-digested
caviar and faded quartet lie in coffins wearing the same finery.
Kenny no longer proprietor is back in Queens living with his mom.
Estelle took the diamond to pawn at Tahoe and got back her job.
One night Kenny dreams pastrami and pickles ripening with dill
in an oak barrel with a slice of poppyseed cake on top.
He's a boy looking in the window of Ratner's amazed and drooling
and he wakes to a fever of barreling dill and fennel he proceeds
to fill with his mom's kitchen his room and his brother's and the yard.

A year later with brother Zack he opens on Independence in Queens
there are bowls of pickles and baskets of hallah on every table
on the blackboard menu liverwurst with red onions on rye bread.
Fluffy matzo balls float like balloons in gold chicken broth.
At the 15 year-reunion hi-school at the deli the eyes in the heads
of his high-school pals glisten with delight over round bellies.
Kenny's delis spread then all over America even in rib-country
Kansas Texas and other pork lands. His sophisticated odes
to the miniscule briefly taken up by sous-chefs in once booming cities
don't last long past Kenny's and the market's collapse
and now they work almost gratis to learn Kenny's pastrami
to feed the appetites of large men and loud women wearing zircons,
making new holes in their belts after every meal.
Such story, never complete without a grand moral, Kenny provides:
"The child at Ratner's window always knows more than James Beard."

the redhead at the piano

is that the redhead with unruly hair
beating the piano like it was a bad kid
in a 1930s alabama classroom?
yes that is the redhead beating the piano
on stage in front of the frayed brown
velvet curtain behind which eerie moans
mix with brief gales of laughter.
the barry white of poetry is moaning
with jaws locked over his open mouth
pants around his ankles as desdemona
on the floor is laughing her own pants
off from an earlier song that just didn't
come off. there are days when actually
all four protagonists relive the scene
as if it was only a few moments ago
not in the last third of the twentieth century
when bravado poetry oral sex and the piano
have a moment. let them have it, ok?

the seventies

for Allan Kornblum

we hate academicism translatese and new urbanism
as embodied by any number of adherents.
all isms are encouraged to take a hike even
if we ourselves put an ism on ours like a tail
on the donkey. don quixote's. there is
one hotdog left. darrell was talking so much
he forgot to eat. his cat just stole it. that's
catechism for you. darrell was sort of catholic
come to think of it. and buddhist. and zen.
he'd have learned calligraphy if he'd had a master.
alas. all of darrell's masters were oral. ink was jism.
and expensive to boot. thieving cat, zen realism.

1978: the night before

for sandie castle

the problem with sex is that it makes you sleepy and you eat sweets
that make you so fat you'll never have sex again except sideways
the futurist said to himself listening in wonder to sandie and rachel
who rolled in in the morning of my youth into my room at the chelsea hotel
saying so fat so fat so fat over and over until they fell asleep laughing
i'm not sure who was president in those days it must have been a good one

requiem for a great bookstore

for the Wilentzes

The 8th Street Bookstore was a writers' bookstore a nest
of snob-clerks like myself a court for writers approved
by our high lit bar at the bar afterhours
all of the greats were in our 1967 rolodex
names followed by numbers money they owed Ted
and Ely for the snob-lit they bought from us
not one writer dared to buy something we frowned on
for that they went to the Paperback Booksmith across
the street where the bottom line was less severe (and there
were girl clerks less rigorous and curvier there).
Anaïs Nin came once leaving her chauffeured car waiting
she asked for *The Partisan Review* featuring her
we adored her instantly she was a narcissist like us
we loaded her illegally parked car with veneration
and the very latest in the american avantgarde she missed
all that time in Europe with her famous friends.
Oh the books that would go to bed with Anaïs Nin! That night!
Imagine! I did. I hadn't published anything yet but I nonetheless
loaded my future books in the trunk of her car I was sure
that she could read them even if they didn't yet exist she was Anaïs Nin
I was a curly-haired poet I found prose a low form of bourgeois pap
but I forgave Anaïs because she had made a poetic halo
from the brilliant minds whose bodies she had used for study.
Most of those people were dead and legendary already just like
we were going to be soon but didn't know it yet. Sure enough
the 8th street bookstore died when Ted refused to hire women
on the grounds that book boxes were too heavy for them,
being mostly hardcovers of complete works by great men.
The budding and ferocious feminists of the seventies targeted
our store for protests, the second all-male preserve after McSorley's
beer bar on 7th Street next door to where Paul Blackburn lived.
Ted gave in and hired women who could lift boxes but then

the employees decided to unionize and the razor-thin edge
of profit went away, and the greatest bookstore in the village with it.
Soon, though we didn't know it yet, books themselves would die.
Our high culture dispensary became a shoestore at first. A number
of other shoestores followed. Then the place was a poster store.
America worked in cahoots with the avantgarde to kill the book
by making it both a god and a cause and something too heavy to carry.
In our avant-understanding of all things we blamed the kitsch
of big publishing greed for the dying of the book not knowing
that a Dark Knight was rushing through the zeitgeist toward us all.
Jeff Bezos rode his Amazon all night and entered Troy to bring the end:
box-weight issues became a sea of tissues at the bar from which
our army surplus selves were soon expelled by high-heeled
pumps and alligator boots filled with C-notes.
In the window where Nin Roth Mailer Olson and Cage once primped
faux-hippie posters buttons and hookahs clowned their kitsch.
The window looked already dusty as tech accessories filled it up.
The vegan restaurant next door ran out of rice. Its palm-reader
looked at my hand and said Go West Young Man and there I went
with the unrepentant avantgarde in tow shouldering her heavy boxes
of minuscule poetry pamphlets lifted from the never-to-be-equalled
poetry section upstairs at the 8th Street Bookstore where Anaïs Nin
still shopped with an eye to the curly-haired poet setting history on fire
with the torch of his pen (pants) that the girl clerks in The Paperback
Booksmith appreciated more than the immortal Nin.

Anselm Hollo

for Jane Dalrymple

Sunday at 8 p.m. or Monday, Wednesday, Friday, or any
day at 8 p.m. we will use punctuation then drive to London
in 2013 to see Anselm, Gunnar, and Tom read again the
unpunctuated past when poets would rather die than drive.
When the clerk in the British walking-cane store barraged
us with questions of height, weight, and leaning direction
pointing out the cheapest cane cost the same as a cheap car,
we rolled out laughing. The cane would have been a gift
to Anselm who greeted our story with his uproarious laugh
worth a Ferrari, the gift that beat back the centuries
with modern insouciance. Shortly after returning
to the States he died. His laughter was worth all the fancy
canes twirled by the dandies of yore. Thank you, Jane,
and be sure, my friends, to walk into any silly London store.

día de los muertos

The other day I found an old beat-up address book.
It was cleaning up time.
Things clutter and you have to say goodbye.
The older you get the more things you have to say goodbye to—give away or
throw out—and not just things, but categories of things:
whole drawers full of letters and manuscripts
—get some cash for them if possible—
hundreds of books
including those signed "to my best friend"
and in the end, books by friends who died
as Jim Carroll put it, après Ted Berrigan,
"friends of mine who died,"
"they were my friends   and they died died died"
and elders   your parents   they died
these people   friends   parents   you can't sell to library archives
you can't give away   you can't throw away
but you do have to get rid of them
if you're going to live your own life
people   friends   parents
they've gone away   you keep all you need
in pictures in your head
     talking with others still alive
        who knew them
you have to get lighter
        to prepare for your own death
god forbid that you become the pack-rat of your own memories

you know
     that when you die people will get rid of your own books
             be sure to to tell them as Ted did:

People of the Future
while you are reading these poems

remember
you didn't write them
I did

you can't do any better than that
you say I, me, the only one like this, I wrote this poem and there,
    it's not universal, it's not yours,
     it's not even a fancy or an image or a poem
it's just me
    that's all
I wrote it

so I was looking through this old address book
    with a view to getting rid of it

the letters of the alphabet staggered out on tiny plastic flaps
  it was easy to look up anyone
    whose name started with any letter from A to Z
     I felt affection
     some dead friends were carefully crossed out
      with a single line of black ink
but I could still see their names, address, and telephone number
  I could see their "I" still

how different from the constantly changing and improved Contacts
    that I now keep on a bunch of devices
     computer tablet iPhone
      a seemingly spacious and ubiquitous list
that can accommodate in addition to phone numbers and physical adresses
    email and web addresses and notes
that increase their volume but not their importance
  or quasi-importance as in "he's a dick but he can get you a grant"
or "she was something!"
these notes
    not enough for a novel but rudimentary efficiency
     maybe even a skeletal psychological profile

I use Gmail
   so these Contacts
      unlike the addresses in my old book
         are coveted by others who want "access" to them
they want them so they could sell us something
    so they could merge them with others maybe millions of other people
who could then all be sold something
      Gmail added all people who wrote me emails
          the whole fin de 20th and start of the 21st century
             people and institutions
even people who wrote to me while they wrote to hundreds of others
    they too were on my lists of Contacts
and charities   pleas   causes   kickstarters   free poetry free everything
    business associates
       or no-business associates
         or none-of-my business associates
           people I never knew I needed to know
contactable any time with names addresses home and business numbers
          emails   websites   blogs
        multiplied
         masses of names
I had to search hard now for my friends
in the Contacts lists of
"friends"
"so-called friends"
"maybe friends"
"fans"
"poseurs"
"masqueraders"
"useful in a pinch"
"radio people"
"publishers"
"whiners"
"annoyers"
"media requests"
"gigs that pay"

"gigs that don't pay shit"
    the names often overlapped
and I remember how it felt bad if not right down evil at first
    to separate them this way.
I agonized over whether a person was a friend or a fan, a human or a robot.
Many robots with human names seemed to be fans or friends
but I didn't remember them
was it my memory?
Or was it all a mise-en-scène
some fake bullshit conducted with familiarity
through this spider-web of Contacts?
In my early G-spot mail naiveté
I barely noticed when every new app I hipped up my iThings with
    asked to use my Contacts
I realized to my horror and too late
    that the iDevice was giving Twitter Dropbox Walmart Facebook
      the police the Surveillance State Chinese and Russian Spies
        and whoever else cared
          all my Contacts
I started deleting names and categories then
but then stopped
    it was useless   it was too late
      my Contacts were already out there
        for anyone with Google maps to find and annoy or kill
        or do to whatever they felt like to them
I'd let them into my electronic address book
    where they lived on and will live on forever
      on a multitude of devices
      among millions of others
        and among them were many
          people who had died
it just didn't matter if I crossed them out with a single black line
    or whether I remembered them or not
      they would live on forever on other lists
Contacts was just another way to turn an "I"
    into "we"

no "I" wrote poems to the future
the future made sure that "I" was just someone in Contacts
"I"s die but Contacts never do.
The dead   the once deleted
       continue a haunted existence as members of "we"
           used by vapps to sell them shit
the dead have one advantage:
they have no computers
and they have no money.
Will that stop salespeople?
     No.
         In the late 19th Century and early 20th Madame Blavatsky
               a psychic   promoted with great energy
                    an inter-regnum computer
                        that invoked the dead
to make a bridge between them to the living
she sold mediums   ouija boards   magnets   stage sets
        and something called "ether"
we now call "bosons" or Higgs-bosons
        we know that there is no empty space: it's all filled by bosons
weightless things like protons neutrons quarks thoughts and ideas
        get heavy (expensive)
they gain weight while passing through bosons.
Some things get so heavy when they hit bosons they collapse.
These collapses account for 60% of the failure of mediums
        to zero in on precisely what the living kin of the dead
            need to buy in order to placate them
                candles aren't enough any more
                    just like a doll or a truck isn't enough for a kid at Christmas
                    kids now want iPhones with Contacts

in effect there are no longer any people   dead or alive
     there are only social networks
          selling each other things
there is even a "social network" composed entirely of the dead
          who share their own dead Contacts

weird addresses and sets of numbers
    that are hard for us to algorhythmicise or algorhyme
      but you can be sure you're on all the lists

Blavatsky's medium-contacted dead were LOUD motherfuckers.
Blavatsky quotes Roger Bacon on a supernatural event some centuries ago:

"Presently was such excellent music, that they all said they had never heard the like... Then there was heard a still louder music and four apparitions suddenly presented themselves and danced until they vanished and disappeared in the air. Then he waved his wand again, and suddenly there was a smell, as if all the rich perfumes in the whole world had been there prepared in the best manner that art could set them out. Then Roger Bacon having promised a gentleman to show him his sweetheart, he pulled a hanging in the king's apartment aside and every one in the room saw a kitchen maid with a basting-ladle in her hand." The proud gentleman, although he recognized the maiden who disappeared as suddenly as she had appeared, was enraged at the humiliating spectacle, and threatened Friar Bacon with his revenge. What does the magician do? He simply answers: "Threaten not, lest I do you more shame; and do you take heed how you give SCHOLARS the lie again!" Blavatsky goes on to say that *"we are informed by English correspondents of the Theosophical Society that we have heard strains of the most ravishing music, coming from no visible instrument, and inhaled a succession of delightful odors produced, as they believed, by spirit-agency. One correspondent tells us that so powerful was one of these familiar odors—that of sandalwood—that the house was impregnated with it for weeks after the seance."* (Works of HP Blavatsky, Loc 1486 of 70329) on Kindle)

I'm not sure why Bacon, having conjured music, dancers, and perfume, had the need to reveal to his no-doubt paying spectator his humble mistress, but Bacon was a magician in control of the device of ghostly, or ghastly, communications, and part of his use of this instrument was mean satire of the kind we often encounter now in the blogs and comments of our current internet. That is to say, a good deal of the loud old internet that Blavatsky and Bacon extolled, was dedicated, just like ours, to the venting of venomous opinions, gratuitous insults, and an all-out invasion of privacy to and by all Contacts. That spectator, whoever he was, must have felt that if the music, dancing skills, and the wondrous sandalwood scent of his mistress, could so easily be shared by everyone in possession of a Bacon computer, his exclusive enjoyment of her was far from exclusive. Her

Contact was on a hell of a lot of lists. Everyone with profit-making intent or just kinky ideas, could use her. Now since we are all living in Jeremy Bentham's glass house, what's the point of any disguise? Why wear anything? Take off your wigs, please! Then your underwear.

Laura and I were once King and Queen of the Krewe du Vieux in New Orleans. Carnival is an ancient means to confuse the arithmetic of computers and to confuse Contacts. Carnival preserves a bit of privacy within Chaos, but the Day of the Dead preserves also your Contacts. Only Carnival restores through public noise the specific gravity of particular dead people without giving away their whereabouts.

Names deleted from my old address book, thank you for not becoming Contacts!

Oaxaca Día de los Muertos 2014

a bookstore in hay-on-wye

for Arnold Wesker

In a Tudor castle now a vast used bookstore in Hay-on-Wye I came upon a mid-19th century library of one William Terrence Wordling sold together by the estate to eventually be shelved alphabetically by a clerk who had not read the books. Other shelves held books authored mostly it seemed by British surgeons vacationing abroad, or ministers in search of caves. I pulled at random now one then another of this horde of a century of travel to places that wars had wiped off the map of Europe. In one of Wordling's I was startled by pencilled marginalia in a hand so tiny it defied my eyes. I used the magnifying glass of my Swiss-does-it-all tool: pressed it to Wordling's notes and found that they were—in Latin! A pretentious clergyman, I thought. Latin, a language already very dead the year of publication, the year when Napoleon was defeated at Austerlitz, the same year Jacques-Louis David finished his portrait. A language killed again many times in subsequent map-shredding wars. I read in my own primitive school-poor Latin that got suddenly and for no good reason better. I started to fall under Wordling's spell. I didn't see evening fall. The bookstore clerk apologized for the hour. He needed to shut the castle down. I made a deal with him: "I'll give you my Rolex watch," I said, "and I will be here when you come back to open the store." He demurred—a bit. A Rolex for a mad student of marginalia in Latin inside travelogues of little interest, hmmm. "We open late in Wales," he said, "you might be here all night and some. It could be afternoon before I open the castle gate again." "I've had three espressos," I told him, "I have no objection to time, I eat no breakfast, I've had your English fish-and-chips yesterday, a month's worth of calories of me, but this marginalia, " I tapped Wordling gently, "interest me more than food. I'm not afraid of ghosts, I'm sure this castle has plenty. My cousin lives around here, he can vouch for me, goodbye." He took my Rolex and was gone, leaving me a lantern to read by "because the electric bill" he apologized "is more per month than all the books I sell, for all the hype for Hay-on-Wye." I read William Terrence Wordling's densely annotated Latin into the night. His notes did not concern at all the page on which they were written, or any of the printed text. I found not one shred of a connection to the matter of the books he wrote in, as if he'd chosen them on purpose for their indifferent content, though he had authored them in print. The marginalia referred only to itself, it was a book of its own, a work of occult philosophy shot through with equations. When the clerk opened the castle that afternoon he found the bookshelf empty, Wordling's books gone.

He'd often feared something like this.

No trace of the bearded American who had just simply disappeared.

the ausländer & the summer of love

I was the ausländer who wrote that novel
suffering and injustice
the alleviation of
is literature's only value
unless one values
the pure escape to a place
so impervious to cruelty
only a very tall hierarchy
can breach it but it never will
because we have buckets of oil
burning and ready to pour
on the first head we see over the wall
we now value being awake
for that sort of thing
we made a kit of it I'm selling it
it's a pop-up castle in a book
"we are constantly under attack"
andy warhol c. 1974

bookstore for sale

I got a message out of the blue where most messages
come from these days.
How would you like to buy a bookstore?
the out of the blue message said
not just any bookstore
but the most distinguished bookstore in jerusalem
the stein bookstore on king george street
frequented in the past by saul bellow and yehuda amichai
and in the present by our most brilliant young writers
a bookstore filled with new old and rare books
unlike any other in the city of books
jerusalem where the Shrine of the Book is located
jerusalem where books are so important they start wars
jerusalem where books are currency worth their weight in flesh
and are a lot weighter than the screen holding your e-books
but for all that the stein bookstore is for sale
it's cheap for the money
if I had it I would buy it
you get a square of the blue sky of jerusalem with it
a square with a cloud on it
a cloud an angel sits on reading a book

oz: the bees are dying

Associated Press, 2007: The bees are dying. The bees are dying of a virus from Israel. Every Rosh Hashanah we gather to eat apples and honey to usher in a sweet new year. Where the hell are we going to get the honey if all the bees are dying? Of a virus from Israel? Scientists, please stop feeding the antisemites. I'm not a big fan of a pre-ordained Apocalypse and I reserve the right to any kind of end of the world I can imagine. Writers have been imagining any number of world-ends from cataclysmic to comic, but none of them panned out. The most popular, The Gospel of St. John, added to the New Testament over the protests of many theologians, does have bees in it, or black honey, or bitter books that when eaten taste like honey in the stomach. No, I haven't been living here very long, but there is something about the little town of Bee Branch that really cheers me up.

They Want In

There is a line in front of my archive as long as the bread
line in my commie past when my mother sent me out
in the dark and the snow before school, for news. If I got
the bread, fine. If not, the news was the thing. There was
no newspaper. There is no newspaper now either, and I don't
eat bread because it makes you fat. The new line is there
for something else. I don't know what. Maybe air conditioning.
But it's a real anglo line: people behind people in good order.
The Latins don't know lines: they tango and twist ahead, a dance
older than the things they want from the almighty vendor.
In other countries you might see a mob milling in a bath of talk
while executing the complex ballroom dances of the needy.
Whatever the form the window always shuts down just as they
arrive in front of it. For my exegetes it's always closing time.

how chaos works: the wearing away of affections
by techno-golems

supernatural bodies are supernatural-looking
they embody a nonhuman power
they have to shape-shift to fully manifest their draw

they may or may not have once been human
they are aliens the alien has no center because he is the center
the center looks continually for something to take its place
the alien's chief desire is to abdicate

what are stories? they are aliens who unfold
their bodies to gain human attention
but seduction is work: we don't want to work
any longer. we live in utopia, we want stories
told by numbers: let the accountant do
both the counting and the accounting.
the electronic storyteller was born of numbers
to tell stories by numbers so that the human ease itself
into a different being perhaps a honey-tongued superhuman.
language and superhumans are born at the same time
rogue pals in communication, rebel narratives
of constantly one-upping technologies of occupation

stories argue communication like Jews argue Jews

ADAM WAS A TYPO

jews

God created Jews to sing His praises. There are no bad Jews, only Jews who sing differently than other Jews. Is the pitch-perfect singing Jew different in body from the unconsciously off-key Jew? And do the atheist and the blasphemer sing? How? With words. All words are songs of praise to God. What about the mute illiterate Jew? He sings from his Jewishness because the whole Jew is a praise-singing instrument. The body of the Jew is different from the body of the non-Jew because it is soaked in this praise stuff from the first flesh.

BREAKING THE RULE

1. Isaiah to people still milling around after the performance

Ok, the Lord wants us naked when we die
devoid of pride craft culture kinkiness and hubris.
It is His revelation that we are His greatest lie
& a mistake of making, some kind of radio interference
with His own reflective self-loathing. This is direct from Him.
He's not just getting His strings pulled by me, humble Isaiah
craving an anklet nose ring leather gloves a linen vest a credit card
and a table for two at Daniel's, which is anyway forbidden
for having lost a star. But can't I, Lord, have a bit of splendor
in this shabby universe, before Your news becomes true?
Pray let me go broadcast but once wrapped in all this art!
And may this offering suffice to escape the tyranny of your Voice.
Anybody here going my way to some slum that escaped His notice?
I shouted the End to everyone here already, laryngitis is my prize.

2. G-d, looking with some amusement at the candy-wrapper-littered stage after His prophet's speech:

Oy! another messiah fishing for new melodious bile!
Doctors we need not another hairy one of those!
Not another putz yelping at the corner of pilshmoof and yada yada
hoping to scare a debutating goyess out of her clothes
into his bed of naked derridada! Better I'd made a sasquatch.

116

It rains messiahs every time a jewish boy reads too much.
A hard putz may amuse me the lord but something in my guts
tells me that satan squats in every book   between each letter a dybuk!
Listen to this mother (picks mother at random): "I made him
seven boys (not to speak of dinner) and the trouble just grew.
Five doctors, a computer geek, and the required prophet Isaiah
who took after you, his father, but you called him the Other!"
I'm preening in the mirror laughing double at Isaiah's poor mother
spinning out My inspired world from matzo flour!

3.

Having given the sonnet form a lot of thought, Isaiah reflected that, while it was adequate to the lofty anger and the incandescent eschatology he thought he owed his Subject (whose Subject he was), it was not suited to the minutious examination of the Lord's proscribed articles. He thus decided to take these things in the order that they had been listed, and began with the anklets. At this point G-d took over the examination Himself, and Isaiah froze like a radio that, having coughed its last blip, was turned off (for the time being). Meant to attract the eye by drawing it to the beauty of a tender young ankle, this ornament made from ivory, basilisk plate, inebriated silk worm, gold thread ably unraveled from the lion foot on the pedestal of His own throne, or the human bone of some future poet like the great Max Jacob, for whom G-D had a soft spot, or even from the melted iron that held slaves to their whipping posts, an anklet was more than just ankle eye-candy, it was composed of substances that were of use to the objects and the bodies from which they had been painfully torn. G-D was not against reuse, collage, metamorphosis or transformation, but he believed that these things ought to occur when the originals had spent their utility. Prematurely turning an elephant tusk into an anklet was grievous to the elephant, even if the seductive quality of the anklet would reinforce His command to people To Reproduce (and Multiply.) In the case of the anklet, G-D came to the first of many uncomfortable paradoxes that followed the impetuous creativity of His youth. He had encountered many of these paradoxes as Creation unfolded, and He endeavored to treat them with care, not by FIAT or SONNET (which He could also do), but in the form of the prose poem, saving FIATS & SONNETS for the moment when He was going to reveal true nature, which was (spoiler alert!) the conflict between Utility and Beauty. Keep in mind, the Lord saith to Himself (a mind He had acquired specifically for anklet-thinking) that since I endowed the human I produced with the vanity needed to reproduce, I did so with only half the esthetic joy I experienced in making the human in the first place. When I realized this, I could have still gone back and molded the lump Adam into a not-quite-so-demanding-a-form, and saved myself from the annoyances of poetry. I didn't, and by the time anklets became the human whim that is currently driving Me nuts, it was too late to remold Adam: I was more than half way across the river: the Thing started to worship Me! I couldn't just chuck it! Setting Isaiah off on My behalf was a temporary solution: he would excoriate anklet-wearers to a shame that in due time should give anklets a meaning opposed to ornamentation, such as the diminutive for "handcuffs," thus cancelling the object. On the other hand, which one you'll never guess since I'm multi-handed, both meanings might be accepted by humans in order to increase their pride by adding the skill of crime and the courage of the punished to the lust of their ankles. God sighed (in prose) and began to reflect again on the technology needed to stop the relentless production of human geegaws obtained from the destruction of his Creation. He had purposefully made man to become complicated. It was His own fault. Isaiah was a good tool for cowing the frightened mass of the few humans with fewer tools on earth so close to the time of Creation, but what is He going to do now in the future when anklets had become Hermes-style winglets, tracking devices, time keepers, and image projectors, and as common as onanist crops? The next experiment would have to be the shaping of Isaiah into an anklet for Himself. He would twist the raving Isaiah by his laryngitis-pretzeled voice and set him around His own divine ankle. He would then perhaps feel Himself suffused by sufficient Divine lustfulness to quit thinking about poetics.

4. G-d's stomach, Isaiah's sympathy, and escape plans

Isaiah had a heart, something he made sure to keep hidden.
He felt sorry for G-d overcome by the magnitude of the only
pronoun he knew this far, the "I" that he had so ably ridden
to defeat all the other gods until he found himself so lonely

he fashioned the giant mirror that was his only consolation
until He spotted "anklet," an impedimenta that only
something called Humor might end His absolute dejection
and quell His rabelaisian indigestion to theorizing his Creation

for wanting to know what happened to the gods He ate
after He vanquished them in the heroic-clever mode that was
the model for the epic He imagined would be His trophy-fate.
The old gods were all inside Himself alive but somewhat listless

as would you if you spent years in the belly of a whale à la Jonah.
Still, the gods were alive and had ideas. Some of them started to build
spiral-staired cities in His belly, maze-shaped and equipped with sonar.
G-d's stomach sometimes felt like a new printer cartridge

ready to print, impatient in the dark prison of His deep Escher guts.
But it lacked input, text, or even a sign promising *mañana*.
The swirling twister of old gods inside the mono-G-d was often a *hora*.
Until He saw a use for their energy: he ordered them to write the Torah.

The G-d who vanquished the other gods ordered a book that was
the story of His stories recording the triumph of His Creation!
He set at first some lesser gods to rowing couplets rhymed A-A-B-B
and bade them start composing songs to alleviate His indigestion,

perhaps forever! It would all end in a perfect song, a new Messiah.
A row of youngish gods and demigods aided by angels on a pin
began to set type, under the watch of Krishna, Neptune, Osiris, and Maya
to oversee the writing in languages they were once worshiped in.

Isaiah felt pity for His lonely G-d watching Himself in the cloud mirror
and would have gone on feeling sorry if the mirror hadn't filled with text
like a clear lake rent by the sudden encryption of a wind's furor.
Isaiah saw himself written in God's book as "the prophet coming next."

But just as G-d was having biblio-therapeutic fun with his creative A-list
Isaiah spotted a row of theorists black-robed in forms and numbers.
Ah, You old goat, Your goose is cooked! Here come the Kabbalists!
They're close to finding the timber of Your algebra!

5. The Alphabet, formerly Google

Having delivered his new volley of imprecations for the Boss, and administered
another round of apocalyptic thrashing to the forgetful and godless consumers in
the land of Israel, as well as to the herd of kabbalists, geomancers, and poets who
were born of his resentments, Isaiah felt refreshed, like Lenin after a bath and sex
with Inessa. He allowed himself the luxury of lying sur l'herbe on the hill with a
lunch of cold chicken, a jug of wine, and a joint. In this pleasant postapocalyptic,
postrebellious state, he surveyed the toiling hovels beneath his feet, and thought
about the second object of G-Ds wrath: "the nose ring." He wasn't sure of the
translation. "Nose ring," as he understood it, was not an adornment, but an iron
ring inserted brutally into the nose of an animal in order to pass a leash through.
It was worn only rarely, and usually over the bruised eye of a stubborn bull
resisting direction, or incurred by a sailor in a fight with a porter. He had heard
of savages just outside the gates of Rome, who wore suits made from discarded
bones that Romans threw over the walls after orgies, who fashioned some of
these into nose rings for themselves to look more fierce, but he was certain that
G-D did not refer to them, because they were not of the faith. Israelites did not
put rings in their noses. When they made sacrifices they used the whole lamb
or goat and they didn't wear any of it as either nose ring, hat or pantaloons.
Though it is possible, thought Isaiah, making a mental note to include this in his
next round of imprecations, that some of them slipped a heart, a liver, a pair of
cojones or even a rib, in the folds of their robes during ceremonies, for use later
in black market transplant commerce, or vain ornament. Isaiah shuddered, not
unpleasantly, at the thought of wearing a suit made entirely out of stolen cow

parts. He imagined a pride of lions, a pack of wolves, angry Hindus, and a swarm of vultures following him to the Prophet's Pedestal in the agora, where people gathered for his verbal flayings, and he saw himself raising his ornament-laden arms and wriggling the bone ring in his nose in dismay: the crowd, incensed by his hungry pursuers, would set on the lions, wolves, Hindus, and vultures, and beat them dead with crooked sticks and stones, then tear them to pieces, rip off their clothes, and dress in the bleeding fillets of their bodies, fashioning anklets and nose rings unto themselves, ready to listen again and again to his fiery visions. Marvelous, thought Isaiah, how G-D thinks of everything! Only a moment ago, I did not know what "nose ring" was doing among the anklets and the fillets, but now I am in awe of His far sight: He rightly sees that nose rings are required accouterment of prophet audiences, perhaps of all audiences. Isaiah saw a pullulating throng of future audiences to public events of every kind, including opera, dressed in fillets of cow, proudly jingling their nose rings, moments before they were engulfed by the sudden flames on burning stages. And to think, Isaiah reproached himself, that I could feel sorry for such an imaginative and all-pervasive divine cluster!

It's funny
  but not ha-ha funny that many apocalypses later
    most of which were GPSed mini-Armageddons
        in Megiddo proper
          at the exact moment
  when roaming prophet-hunger reached far to the maya
    a 21st century poet could conceive a stormy but cozy intimacy
        between G-D and his mouthpiece

        backed up by the news-cycle
that G-D often pedalled to Isaiah's shows to hear

I'm taking God's parodic summary of interpretations as true somehow, but it's me (poet) talking. This began as a collaboration with a rabbi, but it didn't work for me. I'd made an ontological error, started from a flawed premise. I'd gone a long way trying to make the error digestible, so some amusing things were born of the mistake. Until I had to stop. Then I broke my rule to never extract my own lines from a collaboration, and kept the amusing things because they were good.

121

Without the live internet interlocutor rabbi, there were still two interlocutors left: Isaiah and G-d (or god). That is in my opinion still too many. If G-d is real, you don't need math. The symmetric beauty of a manufactured universe runs on its own. Without G-d, what's Isaiah for? We need Isaiah to threaten us like we need water in our beer. But let's say he's cabbalistically real, and his name is Alphabet, formerly Google: then Isaiah would be a patch to update the slips of the sixth day when an exhausted G-d, tired of making everything up, cheated: He looked in the mirror and made a creature like Himself and he let it be free and funny unlike Swiss chard (which he spent a lot of time on). Then He would need Isaiah to remind his flawed image that even His imagination has an end. Isaiah was insurance in case He'd transferred to his image defects He knew He had. Until He got tired, all that was needed was fresh air to keep the matrix light and cheap. The cabbalist letter-crunchers who figured out the geometry of his inventions, figured that four Isaiahs were needed to make it all true. They came out of the syntactical cloud with four orthographic symbols, for each of them: a parentheses, an exclamation point, one comma, and a period: the first Isaiah the parentheses was His Doubts, the second was one who celebrated him for making the world go on and amuse Him, the third regretting that He had. These three plus the Comma Isaiah who never finished a curse made four.

6. here come the kabbalists

Orthography came late to language, language came late to numbers,
numbers came shortly after geometry, and all of them
came from G-ds chronology: seven days.
One of the less discussed matters is History,
which is actually the thing that distinguished this Hebrew G-D
from the other gods: His invention of History
was synchronous with his invention of Time.
Once those were in place He no longer needed to work,
so he took the Sabbath off.
Before G-D made anything, He was Nothing Himself,
and could have gone on like that forever,
sated from eating all the other gods, listening to them jabber
in His cosmic belly. There was no entropy. His tummy purred.

The emptiness surrounding the fat belly was all Him.
The emptiness was everywhere the single point of a belly
full of polydeities. The racket within never ceased, alas,
so He made a quiet world to distract Him. And He failed.
His belly exploded. A lot of gods crawled out. Everything fell
back into what it had been born of, over and over.
G-d quickly made History, Time, Chronology, to stem the explosion.
He even made Chronos into a god to keep the others in order.
But with the gods scampering He got hungry again.
And there was nothing to eat. The nothingness stretched forever.
Where shall my daily manna-due come from? He asked Himself.
The empty cupboards of the silent universe said nothing,
but a voice within Him said: Polyphony. Sound. Noise. Hunger.
Yelling. Calling into being Things nameless until spoken
and then present and edible. Aha! His first squeak made a Worm.
Then as his hunger grew He roared and called into being
louder and louder shapes, until sated again but tired
he hummed the human form that looked exactly like Himself.
So tired was He in fact that he failed to swallow it. He slid
into morose slumber. The uneaten Adam roamed through the vivid
and energetic forms of the Beginning spurting divine juice.
Lucky from being the only uneaten thing on G-Ds future screen
Adam bracketed his sleeping and sated Creator inside
his own two-legged form that was His mirror image,
and started to pace, feeling the stirring of a difference,
an appetite for something, just like his Creator had before
he made him. Trapped in Being in a state of hunger, he had
a revelation. He was a point added to infinity, the Thing
that was hungry for not being eaten. This is carelessness for you,
and tiredness too: in a universe existing only to be G-ds food
Adam could never be either sensical or good.
If he'd chosen less ubiquity and more entertainment
he might have gotten away with it. After all, no one was watching.
The escaped gods once eaten could barely see beyond the folds and curtains.
The First Eaten, more numerous than puppets in a threatening mood,
were deprived of the view, no longer able to stare out of His belly button.

7. Adam freelance

Adam curved under G-Ds sleeping shadow felt the desire to make.
He knew that his growing appetite for making was an error
because it carved a new infinity which tired G-D who'd left him uneaten
would never have allowed. Adam jumped on G-Ds belly, ostensibly
to wake Him, but with each leap and thump G-d only turned over
and had another dream, the same dream always, the dream that
He had left something behind uneaten, and that its name was Adam,
and this Adam was and wasn't like Himself, it was a hungry pest
who wanted not food but a hot redhair from a slum in Budapest!
Imagine. This Adam was a horny, real devil, something annoying
with a hairy chest. Still, the Lord did not wake. Adam jumped
and jumped on the belly of the Divine Dreamer like on a mattress
and Adam was a kid. Eventually his jumping made fine holes
in G-ds sleep like light through a sieve. The thousand and oneth time
G-d turned over He dreamt Eve. He gave a Spinning Nothing
in His dream a Something that differed both from Adam
and from Himself, a shapely Whim with Breasts.
He'd eat them both later He told Himself within His Dream.
He made them a garden and a story, too, because they wouldn't
stand still until they used their differences, but when they did
there was no relief. They weighed a ton, the uneaten things,
and still jumped on His belly as they frolicked under a Tree.
Still He slept, leaving the jumping pair wanting and verklempt.
They bothered Him so much He had a Dream-idea that was fun:
he dreamt that the World died. Adam would calm down
and lustful Eve would quit her constant Please, Please, or else,
whatever that Or Else might be. G-D then made Time
run backwards like a film. Adam and Eve believed then
that they were made first in the image of a G-d not yet born.
His Dream-idea was that if they thought the World was there for them
they'd stay so busy eating it, they'd leave Him undisturbed
and stop jumping on his gut. He hoped that out of their own hunger,

these mirror-devils would jump off his tummy and out of His Dream and go find whatever humans eat, canned soup, noodles, duck wings, fish eggs, braised gull, hog feet.

And that's just what happened, saith Isaiah.1 with his mouth full.

Acknowledgments and Thanks

Versions of these poems have appeared in *Spolia*, *Plume*, *Joel Dailey's Fell Swoop*, *Big Bridge*, *Litscapes*, *Janus*, *Van Gogh's Ear*; and in Romanian translations by Carmen Firan in *Scrisul Românesc* (Craiova), Ruxandra Cesereanu in *Steaua* (Cluj), Dan Sociu in *Discutia Secreta* (Arad), and in French by Elizabeth Brunazzi in *Recours au Poème* (Paris).

About the Author

Andrei Codrescu was born in Transylvania, Romania, and emigrated to the U.S. in 1966. He has numerous wonderful books. He founded *Exquisite Corpse: a Journal of Books and Ideas* (corpse.org). In 1983, he taught literature and poetry at Johns Hopkins University, the University of Baltimore, and Louisiana State University, where he was MacCurdy Distinguished Professor of English. He is a regular commentator on NPR's *All Things Considered* and received a Peabody Award for writing and starring in the film *Road Scholar*. In 1989 he returned to Romania to cover the fall of the Ceausescu regime for NPR and ABC News and wrote *The Hole in the Flag: A Romanian Exile's Story of Return and Revolution*. He is the author of books of poems, novels, and essays, the most recent *So Recently Rent a World: New and Selected Poems*, *Bibliodeath: My Archives (With Life in Footnotes)*, *Whatever Gets You through the Night: A Story of Sheherezade and the Arabian Entertainments*, *The Posthuman Dada Guide: Tzara and Lenin Play Chess*, and *The Poetry Lesson*.